THE FIRST IMPRESSION

PERSONAL BRANDING AND CAREER SUCCESS FOR STUDENTS

AF582386

JATIN TIWARI

Copyright © Jatin Tiwari
All Rights Reserved.

This book has been self-published with all reasonable efforts taken to make the material error-free by the author. No part of this book shall be used, reproduced in any manner whatsoever without written permission from the author, except in the case of brief quotations embodied in critical articles and reviews.

The Author of this book is solely responsible and liable for its content including but not limited to the views, representations, descriptions, statements, information, opinions and references ["Content"]. The Content of this book shall not constitute or be construed or deemed to reflect the opinion or expression of the Publisher or Editor. Neither the Publisher nor Editor endorse or approve the Content of this book or guarantee the reliability, accuracy or completeness of the Content published herein and do not make any representations or warranties of any kind, express or implied, including but not limited to the implied warranties of merchantability, fitness for a particular purpose. The Publisher and Editor shall not be liable whatsoever for any errors, omissions, whether such errors or omissions result from negligence, accident, or any other cause or claims for loss or damages of any kind, including without limitation, indirect or consequential loss or damage arising out of use, inability to use, or about the reliability, accuracy or sufficiency of the information contained in this book.

Made with ♥ on the Notion Press Platform
www.notionpress.com

To all the students are striving to create a future that reflects their true potential.

This is for you!

Contents

PROLOGUE

"Success is not about being the best.

It's about always getting better."

– Behdad Sami

Preface

When I started my journey as a college student, I never imagined how powerful the concept of personal branding would become—not just for professionals, but for students like us. College is often seen as a stepping stone to the "real world," but what I've realized is that the journey begins much earlier. The impressions you make, the networks you build, and the way you present yourself today can define your tomorrow.

This book isn't a lecture or a set of commands. It's a collection of lessons, insights, and stories from my experiences over three transformative years in college. As a placement head, student editor, and a passionate learner, I've seen firsthand how personal branding can shape opportunities, open doors, and set you apart in a crowd of equally talented individuals.

I've designed this book to be practical, engaging, and, dare I say, a little humorous. It's not just about building a personal brand; it's about adopting a mindset that pushes you toward success. It's about answering questions like:

What makes you unique?

How can you stand out in a sea of resumes?

What impression do you leave behind?

Whether you're a first-year student trying to find your footing, someone preparing for placements, or just curious about the buzz around personal branding, this book is for you.

I've filled these pages with actionable tips, relatable anecdotes, and strategies that worked for me and my peers. My hope is that by the time you close this book, you'll feel inspired to take control of your personal brand and approach your future with confidence and intention.

Here's to standing out and making your mark. Let's get started!

Warm regards,
Jatin Tiwari

I

Introduction – Why Personal Branding Matters in College

This is not a story, and this is not a command in the book it's all about my experience in these three years of college can't promise that this book will change your life one thing I can promise is it will change your mindset.

Yes, the mindset that says what will happen by doing this, You can skip this step, Do you need to do this right now? Rather than personal branding, this book is to give you a mindset that will force you to get succeed.

According to Google -

"Personal branding is the process of defining and promoting who you are as an individual, and how you want to be perceived by others."

But what do you mean by perceived?

Is it something that people have in their minds about you.?

To some extent, it is correct but the perceived value is also created in the past. Just for an example think about any of the toppers in your batch, what did come to your mind first? A guy with cool body language, fav student of teachers, and many more things. But could you think about this before you get into college?

Of course not, He/she made this perception in your mind through his/her work, networking, and many more efforts. So Perceived value is something that comes up in people's mind just after hearing the name, no matters its the appearance, the confidence, the skills or something else. It is what we feed in people's mind, isn't it?

Your college professors, friends, and future colleagues, I will make the impression the first time they see you, and like that, they will treat you to the rest

The rise of personal branding in today's competitive world.

first, let's start with the obvious question—*what is personal branding?*

Many people confuse reputation with personal branding. According to Harvard Business Review, "Your reputation is made up of the opinions and beliefs people form about you based on your collective actions and behaviors." On the other hand, personal branding is intentional. It's a way to differentiate yourself from the competition while establishing yourself as an industry thought leader. In today's world, it's not enough to be a strong performer. You need to have a stellar personal brand.

Think like an entrepreneur, You are hiring a candidate for an analyst role in your organization, now 2 candidates have come up with the interview sessions,

- You're going through one resume that has relevant exp, certificates and all that you need for that role.
- On the other hand, 2nd resume has the website link of the candidate where he has shown all his work, blogs, past employer experience with a good record.

Now a simple question is who would you prefer? Maybe the first candidate is good but the presentation of 2nd one is more appealing.

You can edge personal branding to -

- Boosts your chances of being seen by employers
- Increases exposure to job opportunities
- Forces you to clarify your unique value proposition
- Positions you as a thought leader
- Fuels professional and personal development

Whether you're unemployed, working for someone else or self-employed, don't underestimate the power of personal branding. It should be consistent, authentic and support your professional goals. While it isn't a process that happens overnight, it's well worth the effort. Once you control how you want to be seen in the world, opportunities will find you.

Takeaways :

- **Your personal brand is more than just a fancy term**—it's how people remember and perceive you, both online and offline.
- **College is the perfect time to start building your brand**—whether it's through projects, internships, or even your social media presence. Don't wait until after graduation to start thinking about it!
- **You don't need to be a social media influencer to have a personal brand**—your unique strengths, skills, and experiences are what set you apart. Own them!
- **Your personal brand is evolving, just like you**—it's okay if you're still figuring out what you're all about. Start small and let your brand grow with you.
- **Networking is key**—and it doesn't have to be awkward. Building genuine relationships is part of strengthening your brand.

Next time someone asks, "*What makes you different?*" you'll have an answer that goes beyond just your GPA.

II

The Importance of Networking

You've probably heard this a thousand times: "It's not what you know, it's who you know." Annoying? but true.

If you are reading this chapter, it clearly means that you want to enhance your network and networking skills. According to MiSha "*Networking is not collecting contacts! Networking is about planting relations*". You should network like you are building your family – People who know what you bring to the table can help you in many unexpected ways. Whether it's finding an internship, getting career advice, or even just learning about cool opportunities, the right connections can take you places.

But, before you start sweating about shaking hands at fancy events, here's the truth: networking doesn't have to be stuffy or formal. It's all about building relationships with people you actually want to connect with. Your professor, your friend's dad who's in marketing, even that classmate who always seems to know about the best internships—these are all part of your network.

Key Lessons from Networking

Networking happens everywhere— When we say networking, the first thought is corporate events or LinkedIn but take networking as a wider term. Think class projects, college fests, grocery stores, PVR, and even coffee breaks. Your next opportunity could be a conversation away.

Be genuine. Forget rehearsed speeches and elevator pitches. Everyone is smart today, and most people can see that you are bothering (buttering) them or interested in connecting with them. So, Be REAL, people connect with you better when you're real. Instead of trying to impress, aim to make a genuine connection.

You're not asking for favors. If today someone is handing me a resume and directly asking for the job, probably that resume will be under the files for some weeks. Networking isn't about handing out resumes or asking for jobs—at least, that is not the right way. It's about learning, sharing, and building trust.

Be helpful. Networking is a two-way street. Look for ways you can add value to others, whether it's connecting them to someone you know, offering insights, or simply being a good listener. "If you want someone's help, you must be able to help them" – As simple as that.

Networking Myths (And Why They're Wrong)

Myth 1: You need to be an extrovert to network.
Nope! Some of the best networkers are introverts because they listen more than they talk. They understand better. It's not about being loud, it's about how long you were in their mind, of course in a good way!!!

Myth 2: Networking is only for businesspeople.
Once I asked a guy, "Why are you still not on LinkedIn?"
He replied, "It's not necessary for me, I'm not doing any business or

something"

Not at all. Networking is about relationships, and relationships are everywhere—whether you're in business, engineering, arts, or even planning to be the next great YouTuber.

Myth 3: You need to have something to offer right now.
Not necessarily. You don't always need to have the world figured out to start building connections. Your curiosity, willingness to learn, and genuine interest are enough to attract to good people around you and establish your positive image in their heads.

Networking in College: How to Get Started

1. Start Small. (From my real experience)
You don't have to jump into massive networking events and ask for numbers. Start by reaching out to people in your immediate circle—classmates, other departments, professors, or seniors. Shoot someone an email or grab a coffee with them to chat about their experiences.

2. Attend College Events – Your potential network is here.
Remember those workshops, fests, and seminars your college keeps organizing? Yes, those are gold mines for networking! Even if it's just a small conversation with the speaker or your peers, you're already on your way. Try to reach out with an affirmative intent. Ask something as their experience can solve your doubts, this will connect the speaker with your mindset.

3. Join Online Communities.
LinkedIn is like the coca seed of your coffee, YES BRO! Quality Matter.
LinkedIn is important, sure, but don't forget about other places like Twitter, Facebook groups, or even Discord servers related to your field. You can easily find like-minded individuals and professionals in those spaces which might be the executives or great leaders of their field.

4. Follow Up. Tried and Tested
Did you meet someone cool at a seminar? Send them a quick

message on LinkedIn or drop an email. Keep it casual—just let them know you enjoyed the conversation and would love to stay connected.

A small story insight –

Once a speaker came into our orientation program after that program I walked to her and asked some questions that could help me to enhance my profile and personal brand.

Later I connected with her on LinkedIn, forwarding two years—she was again invited to the program of our college and she remembered my name, and the feedback she gave to my teachers was that he is good at connection building.

Networking Cheat Sheet: Starter Lines for Meaningful Conversations

1. For Events or Seminars

> “*"I really enjoyed the talk on [topic]. What did you think about it?"*
>
> *"Have you attended other events like this? What's been your biggest takeaway so far?"*”

2. For Meeting Professionals or Alumni

> “*"I'm curious, what inspired you to pursue a career in [industry]?"*
>
> *"What's one piece of advice you wish you knew when you were starting out?"*”

3. For Classmates or Peers

“"Hey, I noticed you've been working on [project/course]. How's that going for you?"

"What's your approach for managing time with all these assignments? I'm always looking for tips."”

4. For LinkedIn or Online Connections

“"Hi [Name], I've been following your work on [topic/field]. I'd love to hear your thoughts on how [trend] is evolving."

"Hi [Name], I'm currently studying [field] and noticed we have a few shared interests. Would you be open to sharing how you got started in [career]?"”

5. For General Curiosity

“"What's your story? How did you get into [field/role]?"

"What's been the most rewarding part of your career journey so far?"”

Bonus Tip: Rather than getting into an interview mode with someone, try to build a real conversation by going deeper into topics. Always end with a genuine follow-up like, "It was great chatting with you. I'd love to stay in touch and hear more about [topic]!"

III

Building a Personal Brand in College

"Tell me about yourself"

It is not just an 'Interview Starter', it is those 3-4 years that you have spent in your college, internships everything. Its just "kya ukhada hai?"

Think of your personal brand as the story you tell the world about who you are and what you bring to the table. It's not just about your grades, it's about the value you add to every interaction, project, and post you make. So, how do you craft this story while you're still figuring things out? Let's break it down!

Identify Your Strengths, Skills, and Unique Value Proposition

First things first: What makes you *you?* What can you do that others can't or you can do better? It could be your knack for problem-solving, your leadership in group projects, your creativity in presentations, or anything. This is your **unique value proposition**—the thing that sets you apart from everyone else.

Still hard to find?

Here's a simple exercise to get started:

> *"Ask yourself, "What am I naturally good at?"*
> *Next, "What do I enjoy doing the most?"*
> *And finally, "What have others complimented me on?""*

Take your time and think! What was the thing you were complicated for? Once you've nailed down your core strengths, these will form the foundation of your personal brand. You want people to associate you with these skills whenever they hear your name.

Before moving forward, you should be clear about your aim, personal goals, and values
Your personal mission and values are the guiding principles behind your brand. It's what you stand for, what drives you, and how you make decisions. When you have clarity of thoughts, Your decision-making becomes clear and straight. This might sound heavy, but it's actually pretty simple. Think about the kind of impact you want to have on the world or the people around you.

How to Define and Communicate Your Personal Mission and Values

Before moving forward, you should be clear about your aim, personal goals, and values Your personal mission and values are the guiding principles for you. It's what you stand for, what drives you, and how you make decisions. When you have clarity of thoughts, Your decision-making becomes clear and straight. This might sound heavy, but it's actually pretty simple. Think about the kind of impact you want to have on the world or the people around you.

Here's a cheat sheet to define your personal mission:

- What do I care about most? (Helping others, creativity, leadership, etc.)
- How do I want to contribute to my field or community?
- What kind of work excites me and aligns with my values?

Once you've figured that out, make sure to communicate it in everything you do. Whether it's your bio on social media or the way you approach assignments, let your values shine through.

Building Credibility Through Leadership Roles, Projects, and Extracurricular Activities

If you want people to recognize your brand, you've got to put yourself out there. A huge part of building credibility in college is by taking on leadership roles, engaging in projects, and being active in extracurriculars. Not only do these experiences showcase your skills, but they also demonstrate your commitment and work ethic.

Take charge at any student club, complete a project that aligns with your goals, or any leadership role – Even if it is small. *Think about it!*

Be Proactive in Managing Your Reputation

Remember, your personal brand isn't just what you say about yourself—it's what others say about you. Think about it: when you graduate, what do you want your classmates, professors, or employers to say about you? Do you want to be remembered as the dependable leader, the creative thinker, or the go-to problem solver?

Pro tip: You have control over that narrative, so be proactive in shaping it. Every interaction, project, and social media post contributes to how others perceive you. Ask yourself regularly, "**Am I living up to myself?**"

IV

Internships and real-world experience

So, you've been sitting in class, soaking up all that sweet, sweet theory. But guess what? Knowing all the marketing models or HR strategies won't matter if you don't apply them. This is where internships swoop in like the heroes they are. Think of an internship as your first attempt at cooking a dish after watching a YouTube tutorial. You've seen the process, you've got the recipe, but now it's time to get your hands dirty and figure out if you can actually make it work without burning the kitchen down.

Internships are more than just work experience—they're the first real-world test of everything you've learned. And the best part? You get to mess up (a little) because you're doing it under someone's supervision.

Why do Internships Matter?

Internships are **gold** for a student. Why?
It's your first chance to turn theory into practice. Imagine learning to drive a car by just reading the manual. Sounds ridiculous, right? You need real-world practice, with someone by your side to shout

"BRAKE!" when you're about to run into a lamppost. Internships give you that safety net. You're not expected to be perfect, but you are expected to learn.

Plus, you get feedback! It's not like the classroom where you hand in an assignment and forget about it. In an internship, you'll see the direct results of your work, get feedback, and figure out how to improve. And trust me, this feedback is worth its weight in gold, even if it's sometimes brutal.

How to Find Internships?

Now, finding an internship isn't rocket science. It's not like hunting for treasure on a desert island—you don't need a map. But you do need to be smart about it.

Here are two simple ways to land one:

1. **Go through your college's placement cell.** This is by far the easiest way. Most colleges (like mine) have a placement department that's basically your best friend when it comes to finding internships. They've got the connections, resources, and contacts with companies who are looking for interns. The placement department is like your internship matchmaker. All you have to do is know your interests, find a match, and swipe right. Boom! You're in.
2. **Search for off-campus internships.** Now, this one's for those of you who want to go rogue. Off-campus internships can be found on platforms like LinkedIn, Naukri.com, and Internshala. It's super easy—just create a profile, browse through the job listings, and start applying. But here's the kicker: when applying for internships, always, and I mean always, read the job description carefully. You don't want to sign up for a "marketing internship" only to spend your summer making coffee runs and photocopying stuff. Make sure the work actually fits your interests and helps you build useful skills.

Maximizing Your PPO Opportunities

Now let's talk about the holy grail of internships: the *PPO.* If you haven't heard the term before, it stands for *Pre-Placement Offer.* This is basically the company saying, "We like you so much, we want you to stick around after you graduate." PPOs are like getting a job offer before you've even started job hunting. It's a sweet deal.

So, how do you land a PPO? It's pretty simple: be awesome. Show up on time, be proactive, ask questions, take on extra responsibilities, and most importantly, *show your employer that you're indispensable.* When the company realizes that life without you would be just a little bit harder, you'll be on their PPO radar.

Leverage Internships to Build Your Resume and Personal Brand

Let's be real: when it comes to job hunting, experience always trumps theory. Imagine you're a hiring manager. You've got two candidates:

1. One has a shiny degree but no real-world experience.
2. The other has done three internships, worked on live projects, and has stories to tell about how they solved real problems.

Who are you going to pick? Exactly. The one with the internships.

Internships add credibility to your resume. They show that you've been out in the wild, facing real-world challenges. And it's not just about padding your CV—internships also build your personal brand. When you can talk about your hands-on experience in an interview, it instantly makes you more relatable and more competent in the eyes of recruiters.

Personal Anecdote: My Internship Experience

When I started my first internship, I was nervous. I walked into the office half-expecting to mess up and get kicked out by lunch. But here's what happened instead: I learned. I learned a ton. I messed up (a little), and asked a million questions, and by the end, I had built relationships with people who taught me things I could never learn in a classroom.

That internship didn't just give me skills—it gave me confidence. It showed me what I was capable of when I applied myself, and it set the stage for everything I did afterward. It also helped me land my role as a placement head. Funny how things work out, right?

Takeaway: Internships Are the Foundation for Your Career

Internships aren't just a box to tick—they're the foundation of your career. They give you the chance to test the waters, figure out what you love (and don't love), and build the skills that will set you apart in job applications. But more importantly, internships shape your personal brand. They give you stories to tell, problems you've solved, and experiences that make you stand out.

So, what's the big takeaway? Don't just do internships for the sake of it. Be intentional. Pick internships that align with your goals, your strengths, and the career you want to build. Because at the end of the day, internships are more than just work experience—they're your first real step into the world.

Here are five popular websites to find internships in India:

Internshala

A dedicated platform for internships across various fields like marketing, engineering, content writing, and more. Easy to apply and widely used by students.

Website: internshala.com

LinkedIn

Besides networking, LinkedIn is a great platform to find internships. Companies frequently post openings for both internships and full-time roles.

Website: linkedin.com

Naukri.com

One of India's largest job portals, Naukri also offers a section for internships in multiple industries.

Website: naukri.com

LetsIntern

LetsIntern connects students with internship opportunities in startups and big companies across India.

Website: letsintern.com

HelloIntern

This platform specializes in helping students find internships, especially in startup environments, across India.

Website: hellointern.com

V

Leveraging Social Media for Career Growth

Social media, often seen as a playground for memes and selfies, is an underrated gem for students. Yes, you've debated whether "Social Media is Good or Bad" in class essays, but as a practical person, let me say: it's fantastic if you know how to use it wisely. It's your open portfolio—a place to showcase your skills, ideas, and personal brand. In 2024, platforms like **LinkedIn, Instagram, and X (formerly Twitter)** will be your golden tickets to professional growth. Let's dig deeper.

LinkedIn 101: Crafting a Stunning Professional Profile

Alright, so let's break down how to create a LinkedIn profile that screams, "I'm the one you're looking for!" This isn't just about listing jobs and degrees; it's about telling your unique story and showcasing what makes you stand out. To help, I'll use snapshots of my profile to show you exactly what works.

Here's a detailed guide with tips for each section to create a LinkedIn profile that stands out:

1. Profile Picture

Description: Your profile picture is the first thing people notice. It sets the tone for how professionals perceive you. A clean, well-lit, and professional-looking photo is crucial.

Tips to Improve:

- Dress formally or business casual.
- Ensure the background is plain or neutral (a wall, blurred outdoors, or a professional setting).
- Use natural light for a bright, clear image.
- Tools: Use Remove.bg or Canva to adjust the background if needed.

2. Banner

Description: The banner is the visual representation of your personal or professional brand. It's a chance to visually communicate your field or aspirations.

Tips to Improve:

- Include a tagline that represents your goals or motto.
- Add relevant icons or images, such as books for learning or gears for engineering.
- Tools: Design your banner using Canva. They have pre-made LinkedIn banner templates.
- Example: A marketing student could create a banner with "Creativity + Strategy = Impact" and an image of marketing tools.

3. Headline

Description: Your headline is a one-liner that appears below your name. It should summarize your professional identity or aspirations.

Tips to Improve:

- Use keywords related to your field. Recruiters search for specific terms, so be relevant.
- Avoid generic phrases like "Student" or "Job Seeker." Instead, add value.
- Example: "Aspiring Data Scientist | Machine Learning Enthusiast | Python & SQL Expert."

4. Open to Section

Description: This section shows recruiters the types of opportunities you're interested in.

Tips to Improve:

- Be specific about roles (e.g., "Marketing Intern," "Data Analyst Intern").
- Include locations where you're open to working.
- Add keywords to make your profile appear in more searches.

5. About Section

Description: This is your chance to tell your story. Highlight who you are, what you've done, and where you're headed.

Tips to Improve:

- Begin with a strong hook: "A motivated marketing student with a passion for storytelling."
- Use bullet points to emphasize key skills or accomplishments.
- End with a call to action: "Let's connect to discuss how I can add value to your organization."
- Keep it concise but engaging (3–4 paragraphs max).

6. Featured Section

Description: Use this space to display your best work. Think of it as your digital portfolio.

Tips to Improve:

- Include links to certificates, project presentations, blog posts, or videos.
- Add work samples like designs, articles, or research papers.
- Update this section regularly with your most recent accomplishments.

7. Experience Section

Description: This section should include all your internships, part-time jobs, or freelance gigs.

Tips to Improve:

- Use action verbs to start each bullet point: "Managed," "Designed," "Organized."
- Quantify your impact: "Increased engagement by 30% through targeted campaigns."
- Focus on results and skills gained rather than generic tasks.

8. Education

Description: Highlight your academic background and relevant coursework.

Tips to Improve:

- Add certifications or diplomas under each educational institution.
- Mention academic achievements or extracurricular involvement.
- Example: "President of Marketing Club, achieving a 20% increase in participation."

9. Certifications

Description: Showcase any professional certifications that add value to your profile.

Tips to Improve:

- Include certificates from platforms like Coursera, Udemy, or Google.
- Add relevant details: "Certified Digital Marketing Specialist by Google, June 2023."
- Keep this section updated with recent certifications.

10. Projects

Description: Highlight personal or academic projects that showcase your skills.

Tips to Improve:

- Focus on outcomes: "Developed a marketing plan that resulted in a 15% increase in sales."
- Add links or attachments to showcase project reports or visuals.
- Mention collaboration: "Worked in a team of 5 to create a mobile app prototype."

11. Volunteering

Description: This section showcases your social responsibility and leadership skills.

Tips to Improve:

- Include specific roles and responsibilities: "Managed event logistics for an NGO fundraiser."
- Highlight outcomes: "Raised ₹1,00,000 for underprivileged children."
- Show diversity: Volunteering with different organizations adds more value.

12. Skills

Description: List the hard and soft skills that are relevant to your career goals.

Tips to Improve:

- Add a mix of technical (e.g., "Python") and interpersonal (e.g., "Team Leadership") skills.
- Ask peers or professors to endorse your skills.
- Prioritize top 3 skills—they appear prominently on your profile.

13. Recommendations

Description: Recommendations are testimonials from others about your work ethic and skills.

Tips to Improve:

- Request recommendations from professors, mentors, or colleagues.
- Personalize the request: "Could you write a recommendation highlighting my leadership during the XYZ project?"
- Give recommendations to others—it often encourages reciprocation.

Quick Pro-Tips for All Sections

- **Keep it Relevant:** Avoid adding unrelated or outdated information.
- **Update Regularly:** Make edits as you gain new experiences.
- **Optimize for SEO:** Use keywords that recruiters search for in your field.
- **Use Analytics:** Check LinkedIn's profile views and insights to see what works.

With a polished profile, you're not just another student—you're a brand.

Building Meaningful Connections

It's not about having a gazillion followers; it's about connecting with the right people.

- **Whom to Connect With:** Start with peers, teachers, and people you've worked with. Gradually expand to recruiters, alumni, and industry leaders.
- **Personalize Connection Requests:** Always add a note. Example:

> *"Hi [Name], I came across your profile while researching [industry/topic]. I admire your work in [specific field] and would love to connect and learn more!"*

Content Creation: Showcasing Your Expertise on LinkedIn

A LinkedIn profile is only as good as its activity. Engaging content positions you as a thought leader and keeps your profile active in the feed of your network. Here's a breakdown of how to approach content creation effectively:

Why Create Content on LinkedIn?

Content creation on LinkedIn helps:

1. **Showcase Your Expertise:** Sharing knowledge builds credibility in your field.
2. **Engage with Professionals:** Interacting through posts fosters meaningful conversations.
3. **Expand Visibility:** More engagement leads to more profile views.

Types of Content to Post

1. Personal Insights:

- Share your experiences, challenges, or milestones.
- Example: "Today, I completed my first live project on branding, and here are the 3 things I learned about consumer psychology..."

2. Industry News and Trends:

- Post updates on your industry and share your perspective.
- Example: "With AI transforming marketing, here's how I think small businesses can leverage this change..."

3. Tips and Guides:

- Share actionable tips for others in your field.
- Example: "5 ways to create a resume that stands out (from someone who's been there)."

4. Showcase Work:

- Use visuals to highlight projects, certifications, or events you've been part of.
- Tools: Use Canva to create visually appealing infographics.

5. Engagement Posts:

- Start a poll or ask a question to spark discussions.
- Example: "Which soft skill do you think is most valuable in the workplace: 1) Communication, 2) Adaptability, 3) Time Management?"

Tips for Effective Content Creation

1. Be Consistent: Post 2–3 times a week to stay active but not spammy. Build a content calendar to plan your posts.

2. Keep It Relatable: Use simple language. Aim for clarity over complexity.

3. Add Value: Focus on providing useful insights rather than bragging.

4. Use Hashtags Wisely: Add 3–5 relevant hashtags to increase reach.

Example: #MarketingTips, #StudentJourney, #SkillDevelopment

5. Engage with Comments: Reply to everyone who interacts with your post to build stronger connections.

30-Day LinkedIn Content Plan for Students

Day	Content Idea
Day 1	Introduction Post
Day 5	Industry Trend
Day 10	Personal Project
Day 15	Infographic
Day 20	Certification Highlight
Day 25	Poll/Question
Day 30	Milestone

Here's a sample roadmap to get started:

Content Creation on Other Platforms

Instagram:

Content Ideas:

- Share behind-the-scenes of your projects.
- Post carousels with career tips.
- Create reels explaining concepts (e.g., "How I improved my productivity in 5 steps").

Balance:

- Combine personal posts with professional ones to show authenticity.

Tools:

- Use Instagram Insights to check what works best.

X (Twitter):

Content Ideas:

- Share short tips or threads.
- Live-tweet your learnings from a workshop or course.

Engagement Tips:

- Follow industry leaders and comment thoughtfully on their tweets.

Hashtags:

- Use hashtags like #CareerTips or #StudentLife for visibility.

By actively creating and sharing meaningful content, you're not just a consumer of knowledge—you become a contributor, and that's what makes your profile shine.

VI

Placement Strategies for Success

Why Placements Matter
Placements are like the final boss level in your college life—years of coursework, assignments, and internships boil down to this. For many, it's the gateway to their dream job or at least the first rung on the career ladder. Let's decode the placement process and ensure you walk into every interview as the best-prepared candidate in the room.

1. Understanding the Recruitment Process

Think of recruitment as a funnel:

- **Stage 1: Application Shortlisting**

Companies typically review resumes and academic records to create a shortlist. They look for clarity in the resume, relevant internships, and projects, and consistency in academics.

- **Stage 2: Aptitude/Skill Tests**

These tests measure problem-solving, analytical, and technical skills. Platforms like AMCAT, eLitmus, or company-specific tests (e.g., TCS, Infosys) are common.

- **Stage 3: Group Discussions (GD)**

Here, recruiters test your communication, teamwork, and problem-solving abilities. Pro Tip: Speak early, keep your points crisp, and try to summarize if the group conversation goes haywire.

- **Stage 4: Interviews (Technical & HR)**

Technical interviews test your subject knowledge, while HR interviews evaluate your personality, alignment with company values, and soft skills.

2. *Preparing for Campus Placement Interviews*

Preparation is your superpower. Here's a 3-step process:
Step 1: Research the Company

- Understand the company's products, services, culture, and recent developments.
- Explore their website, social media, and platforms like Glassdoor to uncover what they value in employees.

Step 2: Build an Impeccable Resume

- Tailor your resume to each company or job role.
- Use action verbs in bullet points (e.g., "Led a team of 5 to organize XYZ event, increasing participation by 30%").
- Quantify your achievements wherever possible.

Step 3: Mock Interviews and Practice

- Participate in mock interviews with peers or faculty.
- Practice answering common questions like:

> “*"Tell me about yourself."*
> *"What are your strengths and weaknesses?"*
> *"Describe a challenge you faced and how you overcame it."*”

3. Personal Branding During Placements

Your personal brand is what sets you apart. Recruiters want to hire people who are confident and reliable.

- Maintain a professional LinkedIn profile and keep it updated with internships, projects, and certifications.
- Carry a positive attitude—what you post on social media and how you interact with peers shapes how others perceive you.
- Dress the part—formal attire can boost confidence and create a great first impression.

4. Common Mistakes Students Make During Placements

Mistake 1: Unprepared Resumes
Your resume is your ticket to an interview. Submitting a generic, cluttered, or typo-ridden resume can ruin your chances.

Mistake 2: Poor Communication in Interviews
Even the best-qualified candidates can lose out due to lack of confidence or unclear answers. Practice speaking clearly and concisely.

Mistake 3: Overlooking Company Culture
Focusing solely on salary and ignoring whether the company aligns with your values can lead to job dissatisfaction later.

Mistake 4: Ignoring Aptitude Tests

Treat aptitude tests seriously—they're often the first elimination round.

5. Personal Anecdote

As the placement head, I've seen it all—the confident star performers, the last-minute warriors, and the nervous wrecks. I remember organizing mock GDs for my batchmates. One friend, let's call him Aman, was terrified of public speaking. After a few mock sessions, he not only aced the GD but landed an internship at his dream company!

What worked? Preparation, feedback, and consistency. Seeing my peers succeed made me realize that placement success isn't just about intelligence—it's about persistence and adaptability.

6. Placement Preparation Guide (Takeaway)

Here's your step-by-step guide:

3-6 Months Before Placements

Research target companies and shortlist roles of interest.

Build a strong LinkedIn profile and resume.

Enroll in courses or certifications for required skills.

1 Month Before Placements

Practice mock interviews and GDs.

Brush up on technical and aptitude skills.

Attend company webinars or alumni networking events.

During the Placement Drive

Stay calm and confident.

Focus on presenting yourself authentically in interviews.

Keep backup options ready—don't pin all your hopes on one company.

VII

Creating a Winning Resume and Portfolio

Your resume and portfolio are the ultimate tools to market yourself to recruiters. These documents tell your story, showcase your skills, and prove your value to potential employers. In this chapter, we'll delve into the art of crafting a compelling resume and portfolio that STAND OUT in the competitive job market.

I have made sections that you need to include in your resume, with detailed inputs.

Crafting a Powerful Resume

Your resume is a snapshot of your professional life. Here's how to make each section count:

1. The Must-Have Sections of a Resume

Contact Information

- Include your full name, phone number, email, LinkedIn profile, and portfolio link (if applicable).

- Tip: Avoid unprofessional email addresses like cooldude@gmail.com. Keep it simple, e.g., firstname.lastname@gmail.com. And ensure your LinkedIn profile is polished.

Career Objective (Optional but impactful)

- Keep it concise—1–2 sentences focusing on your career goals and skills.
- Example: "Dynamic BBA graduate with a knack for digital marketing and branding. Eager to contribute to innovative campaigns in a growing organization."

Education

- Mention your degree, institution, and year of graduation. Include relevant coursework or projects.

> "*Example: "BBA, Deepshikha Kala Sansthan, Jaipur | CGPA: 8.83 Aug 2022 – June 2025*
> *· Recipient of Business Finance Model Exhibition, 2022*
> *· Balaji Wafers Case Study - Research Project and Project on NGO Internship.*
> *· Collaborated with the college placement cell to assist in the placement process.*
> *· Actively participated in and organized college events, while managing and leading teams."*"

Skills

- Highlight technical and soft skills that align with the job.
- Examples: MS Excel, Canva, Public Speaking, Data Analysis, Team Leadership.

Experience

- Include internships, part-time jobs, or volunteer roles. Write 3–5 bullet points per role, starting with action verbs.

> "*Example:*
> ***Marketing Intern | Zielhoch Together***
> *- Designed digital campaigns, increasing lead generation by 20%.*
> *- Conducted market research and presented actionable insights to the team.*"

Projects

- Showcase 2–3 impactful projects, focusing on outcomes and skills used.
- Example: "Created a social media campaign for a startup, leading to a 25% increase in follower engagement."

Certifications

- Include relevant certifications and online courses.

Leadership & Extracurricular Activities

- Mention positions held in clubs, events managed, or competitions participated in.
- Example: "Organized the college cultural fest, managing a team of 30 volunteers."

References

- Include "Available upon request" unless specifically asked.

Highlighting Key Experiences and Roles

1. Leadership Roles

- Recruiters value leadership skills. Mention roles where you coordinated teams, managed events, or solved conflicts.
- Tip: Use quantifiable results like "Managed a team of 15 members, successfully organizing an inter-college debate competition attended by 200+ students."

2. Internships

- These demonstrate hands-on experience. Focus on what you accomplished during the internship.
- Example: "Enhanced payroll management system, reducing errors by 15% during my HR internship."

Extracurricular Activities

- Showcase your personality and versatility. Mention activities that align with the job role.

Building a Portfolio

Even if you're not a designer or artist, a portfolio can showcase your best work. It adds depth to your application and helps recruiters visualize your potential.

1. Why Have a Portfolio?

- It demonstrates your ability to deliver results.
- It makes you memorable to recruiters.

2. What to Include in Your Portfolio

- *Projects:* Academic or personal projects with clear outcomes.
- *Presentations:* Well-designed PowerPoints or reports.
- *Case Studies:* Summaries of challenges you solved during internships.
- *Certificates:* Highlight professional certifications relevant to your field.
- *Videos/Visuals:* If applicable, add visual proof of your work, like event photos or social media campaigns.

3. Tools to Create Portfolios

- *Canva:* For creating visually appealing layouts.
- *Google Sites:* Easy and free for creating online portfolios.
- *Behance:* For creative fields like graphic design.

Customizing Your Resume and Portfolio

1. Tailor Your Resume: Highlight skills and experiences relevant to the job description. Use industry-specific keywords.

2. Adapt Your Portfolio: Choose projects that align with the company's values or goals.

Example:

If applying for a marketing role, focus on projects showcasing campaigns or market research. For HR, include presentations or reports on employee engagement strategies.

Personal Anecdote: Helping My Peers Excel

During my time as placement head, I noticed a common problem: students underestimated the power of a well-crafted resume. I organized workshops to guide them in building professional resumes and portfolios. One of my batchmates, initially struggling with rejections, revamped his resume with my tips. Within a month, he landed two internship offers. This experience taught me the significance of these tools in shaping one's career.

Actionable Tip: Resume and Portfolio Checklist

Resume Checklist:

- Professional headshot (if you want, not necessary) and contact information.
- Career objective tailored to the job.
- Relevant skills and certifications.
- Quantified achievements in experience and projects.
- Grammar and formatting checked.
- **Always use ATS templates for your resume.** It will be helpful in bypassing ATS rejections.

Portfolio Layout:

1. Introduction: A short bio and career goals.
2. Projects: Detailed descriptions with visuals.
3. Experience: Screenshots of campaigns, event posters, or work samples.
4. Testimonials: Quotes or feedback from professors, mentors, or colleagues.

VIII

Crafting a Personal Mission and Career Vision

"A man without a PURPOSE is like a man without a RUDDER."

Imagine sailing a ship with no destination in mind. The waves might take you somewhere, but you'll never know if it's where you're supposed to be. Your personal mission is that rudder—it gives direction to your efforts, helps you navigate challenges, and ensures your journey aligns with your goals.

In this chapter, we'll uncover the power of defining your personal mission and creating a vision that aligns your academic, professional, and personal life.

What Is a Personal Mission Statement?

Think of a personal mission statement as a one-line summary of your purpose. It reflects your values, aspirations, and what you want to achieve. Here's an example:
"To use my creativity and leadership to inspire innovation in marketing strategies, making a measurable impact on brands and society."

Why Does It Matter?

- **Clarity:** It helps you prioritize opportunities that align with your goals.
- **Motivation:** You stay driven, knowing the 'why' behind your actions.
- **Impression:** Interviewers and mentors admire candidates with a strong sense of purpose.

Aligning College Activities with Your Mission

Your mission isn't just a fancy line on paper; it should shape your decisions:

- **Internships:** Choose roles that resonate with your goals. If your mission involves creative problem-solving, find internships in dynamic startups.
- **Extracurriculars:** Participate in clubs or projects that amplify your mission. Leadership roles are a great way to build relevant skills.
- **Networking:** Build connections with people who inspire you or work in areas related to your mission.

Creating a Vision That Sets You Apart

Your vision is a long-term outlook of what you want to achieve. According to google

> "*A life vision is a* ***mental picture of your desired future that can help you make decisions, set goals, and feel a sense of purpose***"

For example:

"I envision becoming a management consultant, solving challenges for Fortune 500 companies while mentoring young professionals."

When you articulate your vision clearly, it leaves a lasting impression in interviews and networking conversations. It reflects your persona.

Personal Anecdote: My Journey Toward a Mission

During my tenure, I realized that helping peers achieve their career goals was what gave me the most satisfaction. My personal mission—to empower others through mentorship and practical strategies—was born out of these experiences. This mission also guided my decision to pursue leadership roles, enhancing both my skills and confidence.

Steps to Craft Your Personal Mission

1. **Reflect on Values:** Write down 3–5 things you truly care about and are concerned about and that you wish to improve (e.g., innovation, teamwork, learning).
2. **Identify Strengths:** List your top skills (e.g., communication, problem-solving).
3. **Set Goals:** Think about where you see yourself in 5–10 years. Break down those into short-term goals because these small accomplishments will help you to stay motivated in the long term.
4. **Combine:** Merge your values, strengths, and goals into a one-line mission statement.

IX

Overcoming Challenges and Staying Resilient

"Success is not final, failure is not fatal: It is the courage to continue that count." – Winston Churchill

Let's face it: we all know that life isn't all smooth sailing, and neither is your career journey. College is like a mini-rollercoaster—exhilarating at first, then stomach-churning as deadlines, rejections, and responsibilities hit. But hey, what's an epic story without a few plot twists?

Welcome to Reality!

Whether it's getting ghosted by recruiters after interviews or bombing your first internship presentation, challenges are part of the package. It's not personal; it's universal. Everyone face these kind of problems. Here's the thing—they're not endings, they're just dramatic pauses before the hero (that's you!) rises again.

Think of that rejection email as a badge of honor. "We regret to inform you" is corporate for "You're leveling up!" So, put it on your imaginary shelf and move on.

On the other side, apart from the career you are going to face a lot more problems, a lot more rejections, a lot more disappointments, some fake friendships, and some distracting auras. But remember one thing **"What is happening inside you is more important than what is happening around you."**

If you feel intoxicated go for some outings, enjoy nature, parks, mountains, trekking, and do other adventure activities. If you're happy, you can make your surroundings happy and vice-versa.

Bouncing Back Like a Pro (Not Like a Yo-Yo)

Rejection? Failure? No big deal. Here's the playbook:

- **Allow Yourself a Day to Sulk:** Cry into your favorite dessert, binge-watch something mindless, or vent to a friend. At least have one good friend that matches your vibe, with whom you can share yourself completely.
- **Deconstruct the Drama:** Why did it go wrong? Analyze without self-pity. Did you lack a skill? Was it bad timing? Find the root.
- **Strategize Your Comeback:** Missing a Skill? Learn it. Lack confidence? Practice more. Setbacks aren't a stop sign; they're speed bumps.
- **Example:** I once applied for a big internship and didn't even make it to the interview stage. Devastating, right? Instead of losing my confidence, I revamped my resume, stalked (professionally!) the recruiters on LinkedIn to understand what they wanted, and bagged an even better role within a month.

Takeaway: Resilience is Your Superpower

The truth is, life will throw spins. Some will knock you down; others might just brush past. Your job isn't to dodge them—it's to hit back, stronger and smarter.

Here's your resilience toolkit:

- Learn the art of recovery. (Pro tip: Keep a playlist of your favorite motivational bangers for when life gets tough.)
- Always ask yourself: What's next?
- Celebrate every small win—even making it through a bad day deserves applause.

So, the next time life knocks you down, dust off your metaphorical cape, fix that crown, and get back in the ring. Because guess what?

You're Unstoppable!

X

Conclusion – Long-Term Personal Branding for Career Growth

"Your personal brand is not a sprint; it's a marathon. The finish line? Endless possibilities."

As we reach the final chapter, let's pause and reflect. Personal branding is not something you just "do" in college and check off a list. It's a journey—a dynamic, evolving process that grows with you. And trust me, it's one heck of a ride.

From the moment you stepped into college, unknowingly or intentionally, you began building your personal brand. Every class you attended, every friend you made, every project you submitted, and even every meme you shared contributed to how people perceive you.

Your Brand Evolves as You Do

In college, your brand might be about being "that hardworking intern," "the creative designer," or "the go-to problem solver." But as you step into your career, your brand evolves. It will now reflect your professional achievements, leadership roles, and the value you bring to the table.

Think of it like upgrading a game character. You start with basic skills, but as you gain experience, you level up. Your abilities grow, your strengths sharpen, and you unlock new achievements. Your brand should mirror this growth—always evolving, always relevant.

Consistency Is Key

Life gets busy—jobs, deadlines, relationships, even Netflix binges. But the key to long-term personal branding is consistency. Every job you take, every project you work on, every interaction you have—these are opportunities to add to your narrative.

Keep asking yourself, "*What do I want to be known for?*" Then make sure your actions, online and offline, align with that answer.

Lifelong Learning

The world changes faster than you can say "AI takeover." Industries evolve, new technologies emerge, and the skills that were relevant yesterday might not be enough tomorrow.

The secret sauce? Stay curious.

- Enroll in that certification.
- Read that book.
- Network with someone outside your field.

Remember, the only thing standing between you and your next big opportunity is your willingness to learn and adapt.

Your Legacy Is Your Brand

Your personal brand is essentially your legacy. It's what people say about you when you're not in the room. It's the impact you leave behind—not just on LinkedIn, but in the hearts of the people you work with, lead, and inspire.

And let me tell you a secret: nobody has it all figured out. Even the most successful professionals are just winging it sometimes. But the ones who thrive are those who keep going. They stumble, fall, laugh it off, and get back up stronger.

From One Student to Another

When I started my journey as a student, and eventually as someone who dared to write this book, I had no idea how much personal branding would shape my life. I've had my share of awkward moments, failures, and "what the heck am I doing" days. But looking back, every experience added a layer to my brand.

So here's my final piece of advice:

- Dream big, but work even bigger.
- Don't just follow trends—set them.
- Treat every interaction as an opportunity to build your reputation.

Final Takeaway

Personal branding isn't just about who you are today; it's about who you're becoming. It's a lifelong investment in yourself. Keep building it, shaping it, and evolving it with intention.

And when life throws challenges at you, just remember: **"You've got this."**

Thank you for joining me on this journey. Now, go out there and be unforgettable.

About Author

Jatin Tiwari is a passionate advocate for personal branding, a dynamic leader, and a creative thinker.. Currently pursuing his Bachelor of Business Administration, Jatin has worn multiple hats during his college journey—from serving as the Placement Head to leading as the Student Editor of the Management Echo newsletter, working with Samsung India, and many other endeavors.

Jatin's experiences organizing campus placements, mentoring peers, and creating impactful content have given him a deep understanding of what it takes to succeed in today's competitive world. He has helped countless students craft compelling resumes, build their personal brands, and prepare for life beyond the classroom.

An avid learner with a knack for marketing and consulting, Jatin has a talent for turning challenges into opportunities. His ability to combine practical strategies with engaging storytelling makes his writing not just informative but also relatable and inspiring.

When he's not brainstorming ideas for the next big project, Jatin enjoys exploring new books, volunteering for impactful causes, and creating content that sparks meaningful conversations. Through his work, he aims to empower students and young professionals to unlock their true potential and take charge of their futures.

"Your brand is your story, and every day is a new page. Make it count."

– Jatin Tiwari

www.ingramcontent.com/pod-product-compliance
Lightning Source LLC
LaVergne TN
LVHW021202160826
845679LV00024B/2208
9798896990093